TABLE OF CONTENTS

THE MIGHTY BUFFALO HUNT

"An excursion train will leave Leavenworth, Kansas on Tuesday, October 27, 1868 for Sheridan, Kansas," the sign read. "Ample time will be had for the great Buffalo hunt. Buffaloes are so numerous along the road that they are shot from the cars nearly every day."

4

A New True Book

BUFFALO

By Emilie U. Lepthien

CHILDRENS PRESS®
CHICAGO

To Margaret Rohwer who shares my interest in the world's wonders.

PHOTO CREDITS

The Bettmann Archive—5, 35

© Reinhard Brucker—12, 31 (2 photos), 32 (3 photos), 45

© Alan and Sandy Carey—Cover, 13 (left), 14 (left), 17, 18, 21 (left)

Detroit Public Library—39

Division of Manuscripts, University of Oklahoma Library—38

Jerry Hennen—20, 41

Historical Pictures Service, Chicago—23, 26

Journalism Services: © Mike Kidulich—43

Kansas State Historical Society—16, 36

Stanley J. Morrow Collection, W.H. Over Museum, Vermillion, S.D.—30

National Museum of American Art, Smithsonian Institution—24 (left), 25

Root Resources:
© Kenneth W. Fink—10, 14 (right), 21 (right)
© Alan G. Nelson—2
© Stan Osolinski—9 (left), 19

© Jim Rowan—9 (right), 24 (right), 28

© Lynn Stone—7, 8, 11, 13 (right)

Cover—Buffalo in winter, Yellowstone National Park

Library of Congress Cataloging-in-Publication Data

Lepthien, Emilie U. (Emilie Utteg)
  Buffalo / by Emilie U. Lepthien.
    p.   cm. — (A New true book)
  Summary: A history of the buffalo/bison in this country, discussing its behavior and population today.
  ISBN 0-516-01161-8
  1.   Bison, American—Juvenile literature.
2.   Bison, American—History—Juvenile literature.   3.   West (U.S.)—History—Juvenile literature.   [1.   Bison.]   I.   Title.
QL737.U53L47   1989   89-457
599.73'58—dc19   CIP
                                                 AC

This round-trip on the
Kansas Pacific railroad
cost only ten dollars.
Trains left from Cincinnati,
Chicago, and St. Louis as
well. On each trip
hundreds of buffalo would
be killed.

This "killing for fun" was one of the many things that killed nearly all the buffalo in North America.

Once there may have been 75 million buffalo roaming North America from the Atlantic Ocean to the Rocky Mountains. But by 1810, none were left east of the Mississippi River. And by 1900, less than 600 buffalo remained in the United States.

A SPECIAL ANIMAL

The scientific name for North America's largest mammal is *bison*. Most people, however, call the bison a buffalo.

Buffalo bulls (males) can weigh more than 2,000

Buffalo bulls are bigger than the cows.

pounds. Usually they weigh between 1,600 and 1,700 pounds. Bulls stand five to six feet tall at the shoulder. They are ten to twelve feet from their nose to their tail. Buffalo cows (females) are smaller. They weigh about 1,000 pounds.

Shaggy dark brown hair
covers their heads, neck,
and hump. Long hair
(often twenty inches long)
covers their front legs.

Both cows and bulls
have sharp horns on their
large heads. Sometimes

the horns were used as weapons against wolves, coyotes, and even each other. Other times the horns were used to tear up the prairie grass to make a dust wallow (hole). Buffalo could get rid

of biting insects by rolling in the dirt.

Buffalo rolled in mud holes, too. The dried mud protected them from biting flies.

The North American buffalo are related to cattle. Like cattle, buffalo eat grass and chew their cud. Early explorers called the buffalo Indian cattle.

LIFE IN THE HERD

Buffalo, or bison, lived in herds. Usually an old cow was the leader of a herd. The cows also served as guards as the buffalo moved across the prairie.

Cow nurses her calf (left). Another buffalo chases a wolf away.

If a wolf or coyote came too close to the cows and their calves, they might attack using their horns.

The buffalo mating season was July and August. The bulls' roaring and bellowing could be

13

During mating season, bulls fight each other (right).

heard a great distance. Calves would be born early the following spring.

In winter the cows and their calves grazed in separate herds from the bulls. The calves stayed with their mothers until well after a new calf was born.

STAMPEDES

Buffalo have a keen sense of smell.

The scent of danger could frighten the herd. Then the herd might stampede. Sometimes the calves and the old, or sick, buffalo could not keep up with the herd. When they fell behind, the coyotes, wolves, and grizzly bears would have a feast.

Nothing could stand in the way of a thundering buffalo herd. Stampeding herds may have been thirty miles wide and sixty miles long.

Trains crossing the Great Plains were often stopped by buffalo herds.

A herd crosses Yellowstone River in Wyoming.

In spring the rivers were
swollen and the current
was swift. If a stampeding
herd ran into the river,
some of the buffalo would
get hurt and drown.

SURVIVAL

With long thick hair to protect their bodies, the buffalo could survive the harshest weather. The buffalo always faced the winter storms. They moved slowly, conserving their

energy. Even though a
blizzard raged for days,
they would not run away.

Sometimes the winds
would blow the snow away
and the buffalo could
graze. Other times they

Buffalo know how to dig through deep snow to get to food.

would swing their heads from side to side and move the snow with their faces. When the grass was uncovered they could graze.

Buffalo migrated hundreds of miles south in winter. As the grasses turned green, they moved

In spring, the buffalo shed their coats (left). The buffalo herds moved constantly. This gave the grasses on the grazed land time to grow back before the herd returned.

back north. In spring they shed their warm shaggy winter coats. In summer the buffalo broke into smaller herds.

The herds would move constantly to ungrazed land.

THE BUFFALO HUNT

The Indians named the buffalo Pte. They believed the buffalo came up from a great hole in Mother Earth. Buffalo supplied the Indians with almost every necessity.

Before a hunt, some tribes held a buffalo dance. The Mandans prayed first to the Great Spirit. They asked, "Great bull of the prairie, be here with your cow." Songs

Mandan Indian Buffalo Dance. The Mandan tribe once lived in what is now North Dakota.

were sung for a successful and safe hunt.

The Indians knew the buffalo always grazed into the wind. This helped the hunters sneak up on the herds.

George Catlin painted "Buffalo Bill, A Grand Peace Warrior (left)."
In Illinois, Indians used fire to hunt buffalo (right).

The Blackfoot Indians chose a strong runner to wear a buffalo head mask and robe as a disguise. When he found the herd, he started a stampede. He drove the buffalo into a canyon or over a cliff. Then the animals were

This painting shows George Catlin, the artist, and his
Indian guide, covered by white wolf skins, approaching a herd.

killed with bows and
arrows or large stone
hammers.

For generations the
Indians hunted the buffalo
on foot. This made it
difficult to kill them. An
unsuccessful buffalo hunt
meant hunger for the
Indians.

HORSES CHANGE THE BUFFALO HUNT

In the 1500s, horses that had escaped from Spanish explorers roamed the prairie. The Indians watched as the horses raced across the plains. Finally they captured some and learned how to ride. Now they could hunt buffalo more easily. They could ride alongside a herd and select the animals to kill.

This changed the Plains
Indians' way of life.
Instead of earth lodges,
the Indians made tepees
of buffalo hides and poles.
The tepees would be
moved from place to place
as the tribe followed the
buffalo herds.

BUFFALO AND A WAY OF LIFE

The Indians killed only the buffalo that they needed. The lives of perhaps three hundred thousand Indians depended upon the buffalo.

The buffalo provided the Indians with food, clothing, shelter, weapons, and tools.

Every part of the animal was used. Nothing was wasted. The hump, tongue, heart, and liver were favorite

Women used buffalo hides to make tepees and clothes.

foods. Dried strips of meat were pounded with fat and berries to make pemmican to eat on long journeys or on the hunt.

Butchering was done by the women. After cutting

the meat from the bones, they bagged it in fresh hides.

Buffalo hides were made into clothing, tepees, blankets, cooking pots, buckets, snowshoes, and boats.

Bones became hoes,

Hides were used to make containers (left) and shields (right).

 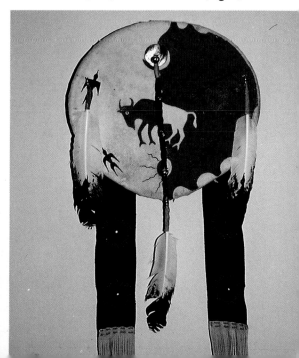

Cheyenne buffalo rib knife (above left), Pawnee buffalo rib sled, doll, toy horse, and teepee (left), and a Pawnee hoe (above)

sewing needles, and scrapers for treating the hides. Ribs were turned into sled runners. Sinews were used for bow strings and arrowhead wrappings. Buffalo hair was braided into rope.

THE GREAT BUFFALO SLAUGHTER

When settlers crossed the Mississippi River, more buffalo were hunted and forced farther west.

Their numbers were reduced as the demand for buffalo meat in the eastern states increased. In the winter, buffalo meat was shipped fresh. In summer it was smoked, salted, or iced. Buffalo hides were sewn into lap robes and sold.

As workers built the railroads across the plains, hunters were hired to supply the crews with buffalo meat. William F. Cody was one of the hired hunters. He could approach a herd on foot and kill more than fifteen buffalo in three days.

When an author was looking for a frontier hero, he picked Cody and nicknamed him "Buffalo Bill." As a result of the

Buffalo Bill

novels, Buffalo Bill became
well known.

A skilled hunter would
kill the old cow leader
first. Without their leader
the animals did not
stampede. At least fifty

A skinned buffalo, "scalped by the white men,"
left on the Kansas prairie in 1872.

head could be killed in a
day. Buffalo also were
being killed for sport, not
food. Their dead bodies
were left to rot on the
prairies. In five years two-
and-a-half million buffalo
were killed in the Kansas
territory alone.

The Indians, especially

the Sioux, opposed the slaughter of the buffalo. Indian uprisings occurred. The slaughter of the buffalo defeated the Indians more effectively than did the United States Army. After they were forced onto reservations, the Indians became dependent upon the government for food and shelter.

Still the slaughter of the buffalo continued. Settlers moved onto the plains.

Buffalo hunters near Buffalo Gap in the Texas panhandle
in 1874. The wooden rack holds buffalo tongues set out to dry.

They sold buffalo tongues
for 50 cents and buffalo
hides for $3.50 to $4.00.
By 1875, great piles of
buffalo hides were shipped
to cities in the East and
Europe. The bones of the
slaughtered buffalo
covered the prairie.

Then the settlers found

During the 1880s, tons of buffalo bones were shipped
to the Michigan Carbon Works in Detroit, Michigan.

that bleached buffalo
bones could be sold for
seven to ten dollars a ton.
The bones were made into
fertilizer. By 1888, even
the bones on the Great
Plains were gone. The
buffalo were almost extinct.

TODAY'S BUFFALO HERDS

By 1905, some people wanted to save the buffalo herds. The American Bison Society was organized. Theodore Roosevelt was one of its leaders.

An Indian named Walking-Coyote brought a small herd to a Montana valley. Other buffalo were added from the small Pablo-Allard herd. From just 37 head in 1908, the herd at the National Bison

National Bison Range, Montana

Range in Moiese, Montana,
increased to about 450.

In 1881, Fred Dupree
started a small herd with
five calves. Part of this
herd was sent to Custer
State Park in 1914. Today
the park has a herd

41

of 950. Other public herds
are found in Wind Cave
National Park, Theodore
Roosevelt National Park,
Yellowstone National Park,
and several other national
parks, state parks, and
reserves. Each place has
only as many animals as
water supplies and grazing
land can support.

Some ranchers have
tried to crossbreed buffalo
with cattle. These animals
are called beefaloes or

Beefalo are part buffalo and part cattle.

cattaloes. These crossbred animals are strong. Like the wild buffalo, they stand facing the wind during winter. They are able to find their own food in winter and will eat snow when water is scarce.

Ranchers in South Dakota, North Dakota,

Montana, Wyoming, and many other states have herds. There are more buffalo in private herds than on public lands in the United States.

There are about 75,000 buffalo in the continental United States and Alaska. Canada has about 15,000. When a range cannot support more buffalo, the surplus is sold to other ranchers or slaughtered for meat. The National Buffalo Association and the

A buffalo bull rests in Yellowstone National Park.

American Bison
Association provide
interested ranchers with
buffalo management
information. They want to
prevent the buffalo from
facing extinction ever
again.

WORDS YOU SHOULD KNOW

bleached(BLEECHT) — made white, or lighter in color

continental United States(kahn • tih • NEN • tul yoo • NYE • tid STAITSS) — the 48 states with connecting boundaries

crossbreeding(KRAWSS • bree • ding) — mating different animals breeds within the same species; for example, cattle and buffalo

cud(KUHD) — food the buffalo forces up from the first of its four stomachs to its mouth, where it is chewed again and swallowed

extinct(x • TINKT) — no longer living

frontier(frun • TEER) — the unexplored region along the border of the farthest known settlement

graze(GRAIZE) — animal-feeding on growing plants in pastures

herd(HURD) — an animal group living together

hump(HUHMP) — animal's raised shoulder area above a curved spine

mammal(MAM • il) — class of warm-blooded animals whose females nurse their young

migrate(MY • grait) — to move from one place to another area in search of a source of food, water, protection

national park(NASH • uh • nil PARK) — government-controlled land preserved for its recreational, scenic or scientific value

pemmican(PEM • ih • kin) — food of dried meat mixed with fat, used as food on long journeys

prairie(PRAIR • ee) — large, flat, uncultivated land

reservations(reh • zer • VAY • shunz) — land set aside by the U.S. government for use of Native Americans

scarce(SKAIRSS) — in short supply

shed(SHEHD) — drop off, as an animal's seasonal loss of fur, wool, or reptiles' and insects' skin

surplus(SIR • plus) — left over; extra

swollen(SWOLE • in) — full, near overflowing, as of a river